50 Classic Cocktails

STEP-BY-STEP

50 Classic Cocktails

Oona van den Berg

Photography by Steve Baxter

SMITHMARK

Many thanks to alcohol aficionados:
Michael Fussell, James Fischer, Nicky Moores, Adrian Heath-Saunders.

This edition published in 1996 by
SMITHMARK Publishers, a division of US Media Holdings, Inc
16 East 32nd Street
New York NY 10016
USA

SMITHMARK books are available for bulk purchase for sales promotion
and for premium use. For details write or call
the Manager of Special Sales,
SMITHMARK Publishers, 16 East 32nd Street
New York NY 10016; (212) 532-6600

© 1996 Anness Publishing Limited

Produced by Anness Publishing Limited
1 Boundary Row
London SE1 8HP

ISBN 0 7651 9753 7

Publisher: Joanna Lorenz
Senior Cookery Editor: Linda Fraser
In-house Editor: Maggie Mayhew
Designer: Eric Thompson
Photographer: Steve Baxter
Stylist: Judy Williams

WARNING
A number of recipes in this book include raw egg. Eggs have been known to carry
Salmonella bacteria which can cause severe and sometimes fatal poinsoning. Use only
the freshest, best quality eggs and avoid using raw egg if you are very young, old or have
a compromised immune system.

Printed and bound in Hong Kong

CONTENTS

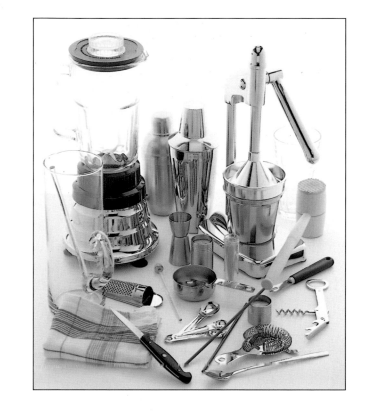

INTRODUCTION

The true origin of the first cocktails is uncertain, but without doubt it was in America that these "mixed drinks" gained the greatest popularity and where many of the more recent cocktail bar favorites were concocted. Cocktails developed in America with bourbon, Southern Comfort and Canadian rye whisky vying for attention. Prohibition was intended to curb drinking habits but only resulted in people ingeniously distilling their own liquors, which were softened by the addition of mixers.

Chic and classic with a strong American twist, the Harvey Wallbanger, the Martini and the Manhattan are here to stay, but more recently, flamboyant tropical cocktails have proved popular. Coconut milk and exotic fruits are whizzed together to create long, frothy cocktails. These concoctions are easily recreated at home now that exotic ingredients are readily available from large supermarkets.

Traditionally, a cocktail is made from only two liquors or liqueurs and the bartender's worth is gauged by making them perfectly, with just enough zing, shaken or stirred to taste. As a general rule, the simpler cocktails and those that are served clear, are just stirred over ice, in a bar glass, before being strained into a serving glass. Drinks that contain fizzy liquids are never shaken, for the obvious, explosive reasons. Cocktails with large quantities of fruit juices, syrups or eggs are shaken over ice in a cocktail shaker; cocktails containing milk, cream, ice cream or coconut milk make wonderful frothy drinks when mixed in the blender.

"Bar speak" is something to get acquainted with: when a recipe calls for a dash of bitters, that means just a shake of the bottle, a squeeze of lemon rind does not mean the whole thing floating in the drink. The rind should be held over the glass and twisted in the fingers, so that the lemon oil drops into the cocktail: the rind is then discarded. "On the rocks" quite simply means served over ice, and "straight up" means served just as it is, in a chilled glass.

At home you can create cocktails with no more than a cocktail shaker, large glass jug, blender and a few essential ingredients such as bitters, plain sugar syrup, and, of course, a couple of bottles of your favourite liquor and liqueurs. Making cocktails is an enjoyable pastime, so make a drink, sit back and savor it!

Liquors, Wines and Cider

Many cocktails contain the same liquors but in different combinations or quantities, so with a small stock of different drinks, a variety of cocktails is possible. For the best results, use the best quality brands available.

Brandy

Brandy is a popular liquor, distilled from grape wines. There are blended brandies available from all over the world, but some of the better and more expensive brandies are French. The two main types of French brandy are: cognac and Armagnac. There is also a range of fruit brandies, or eaux-de-vie, such as peach, cherry and apricot, as well as Calvados, which is a French fruit brandy distilled from apple wine. The American equivalent is applejack. All are perfect for using in a variety of cocktails.

Champagne

Use *brut* (dry) champagne or *méthode champenoise* wines when making cocktails. You'll find that they keep their sparkle a lot longer. Some of the less expensive champagne-style supermarket wines, such as the Spanish Cava, are ideal for mixing with a variety of fruit purées, freshly squeezed fruit juices and syrups.

Cider

A drink made from fermented apple juice. Sweet or dry cider both mix well with brandy and other spirits, as does perry, a cider made with pears. Use perry in exactly the same way as apple cider to make a tasty variation.

Gin

Gin is a favorite liquor and is ideal for mixing with many fruit juices and liqueurs, to create some of the classic cocktails. This colorless liquor is distilled from malted barley, rye or maize. Each brand uses its own very special combination of herbs, spices and citrus oils. Juniper berries give them all their most distinctive "gin" flavor.

Ginger Wine

A golden or green wine flavored, with citrus fruits, floral scents, herbs and ginger. It is sweet but very aromatic and spicy tasting and mixes well with liquors and red wine.

Marsala

This is a delicious fortified dessert wine from Sicily. It is a blend of white wine and brandy and has a sweet caramel flavor. Most people are familiar with sweet Marsala, but are unaware that a dry version with a flavor very similar to sherry can also be bought.

Port

A full-bodied wine, fortified with brandy during fermentation. It comes from the Douro valley of Portugal and is most commonly available as tawny, ruby, white, or Late Bottled Vintage (LBV).

Rum

Distilled from sugarcane and molasses and made mostly in the West Indies, particularly Jamaica, rum is available as dark or light varieties, as well as flavored with coconut and pineapple. It is used in cocktails such as the flamboyant Blue Hawaiian, Mai Tai and Planters Punch.

Schnapps

Generically known as aquavit, schnapps is a popular drink in Scandinavia and Germany. It is a colorless liquor made from grain starch and is also available in assorted fruit flavors such as peach, cherry, blackcurrant, pear and apple.

Sherry

This fortified wine originally came from Spain, but now it is also produced in a large number of other countries such as Greece, Cyprus, South Africa and Australia. It is available in a range of styles: *fino* (pale and dry), *manzanilla* (medium dry), *amontillado* (medium), *oloroso* and *amoroso* (sweetish) and *montilla* (lower in alcohol).

Tequila

Available in clear and golden (aged) hues, tequilas are fermented and distilled in Mexico, from the juice of the agave cactus. Tequila mixed with lime juice and a little salt is Mexico's national tipple. It is also an essential ingredient in the popular Margarita where it is mixed with Cointreau and lime.

Vermouth

A high-strength wine, cooked with a selection of herbs, vermouth is available as extra-dry white, bittersweet rosé, medium-sweet bianco and sweet red. By tradition, French vermouths are dry and Italian ones tend to have a sweeter flavor.

Vodka

A colorless liquor, distilled from rye, malt or potato starch, vodka originated in Eastern Europe. It has a completely neutral taste, which allows it to mix well with other liquors and fruit juices. Steeping vodka with fruits, fresh herbs and spices adds flavor and interest to the cocktail.

Whiskey

There are various types: Scotch whisky, Irish whiskey, the American bourbon and the Canadian rye. Whiskey is distilled from either malted or unmalted grains and can also be blended.

tequila   ginger wine   dark rum   champagne   light rum   sweet vermouth   Calvados

Marsala   schnapps   cognac   vodka   whiskey   port   gin   fino sherry   dry vermouth

Liqueurs

Many liqueurs available today originated as medicinal tonics, and a few were created by monks in their dispensaries. Liqueurs are made from a base liquor with herbs, peels of citrus fruit, spices or extracts from coffee beans.

Amaretto
A sweet Italian fruit-based liqueur with more than a hint of almonds and apricot, used in Hooded Claw and Cider Cup. It's made near the town of Saronno in Italy.

Anisette
Aniseed-flavored liqueurs like the Italian Sambuca and the Spanish anis are often flavored with coriander and fennel as well as aniseed. French Pernod and pastis are also anisettes, often served simply poured over plenty of ice cubes.

Benedictine
Made from an old French recipe passed down by the Benedictine monks of the abbey of Fécamp in Normandy, it is a golden colored, brandy-based liqueur, flavored with myrrh, other herbs and honey. It is an essential ingredient in the cocktail Sea Dog.

Chartreuse
A French brandy-based liqueur made from honey, herbs and spices. Originally made by Carthusian monks at La Grande Chartreuse monastery, the green liqueur has more alcohol than the yellow variety, which is flavored with oranges and myrtle.

Cointreau
Sweet and syrupy, it is a colorless liqueur with a strong aromatic orange flavor and is often served poured over ice.

Cream Liqueur
A mixture of cream, liquor and flavoring, such as Bailey's Irish Cream.

Crème de Cacao
A sweet liqueur originally made with cocoa beans from the Chouao region of Venezuela, it has a cocoa-vanilla flavor.

Crème de Cassis
A brandy-based blackcurrant liqueur produced in Dijon.

Crème de Menthe
A very sweet, peppermint-flavored liqueur, it also includes cinnamon, sage, ginger and orris and has strong digestive properties, which make it an ideal after-dinner drink.

Curaçao
An orange-flavored liqueur, similar to Grand Marnier, which was originally made from the dried peel of oranges from the island of Curaçao in the West Indies. It can be blue, as used in Blue Hawaiian, white or dark orange-brown in color.

Drambuie
A Scottish malt whisky-based liqueur, tinted with herbs, heather, honey and spices. Often used in after dinner coffee.

Galliano
A golden-colored herb liqueur, produced in Italy, and flavored with licorice and aniseed.

Grand Marnier
A French curaçao, based on extracts from the bitter bergamot, orange and brandy. It is similar to triple sec, curaçao and Cointreau.

Kahlúa
A rich, brown liqueur from Mexico. Although coffee-based like Tia Maria, Kahlúa is quite different in style and is popular in the USA.

Kümmel
This caraway and fennel-flavored liqueur is made mostly in Holland.

Southern Comfort
This American liqueur has a bourbon whiskey base and is flavored with fruit.

Tia Maria
A Jamaican liqueur made from rum, Blue Mountain coffee extract and spices. It can be used for a less sweet version of Kahlúa.

COOK'S TIP
Make sure your cocktail cabinet is stocked up with a few of these essentials.

Southern Comfort   Kahlúa   Benedictine   crème de menthe   Grand Marnier   Tia Maria   Drambuie

Cherry brandy

Galliano

Crème de cacao

Cointreau

Blue curaçao

Anisette

Amaretto

Cream liqueur

Green Chartreuse

Mixers and Juices

Whether a cocktail is shaken or simply stirred, it is the juices and mixers that provide a drink's length and body. After all, where would the Bloody Mary be without tomato juice?

These additions to the cocktail should always be as cold as possible. Juices are best if they are made from fresh fruit but, failing that, opt for the better quality, ready-squeezed versions which are not too sweet.

Apple Juice
Available still or sparkling and either clear or cloudy. Always choose a juice with little or no extra sugar or preservatives.

Bitter Lemon
A non-alcoholic fizzy mixer – good with all white liquors. It is made from carbonated water, lemon, sugar and quinine.

Coconut Milk
Used in tropical cocktails, unsweetened coconut milk is available in cans, or in a powdered form. The powder requires dissolving in hot water and then should be left to cool.

Cranberry Juice
A tangy and refreshing fruit drink, available in cartons and glass jars. The regular cranberry juice mixes well with spirits; other cranberry juices, mixed with raspberry or apple juice, offer further delicious flavor combinations.

Ginger Ale
Available in several varieties: dry, Canadian dry and the slightly

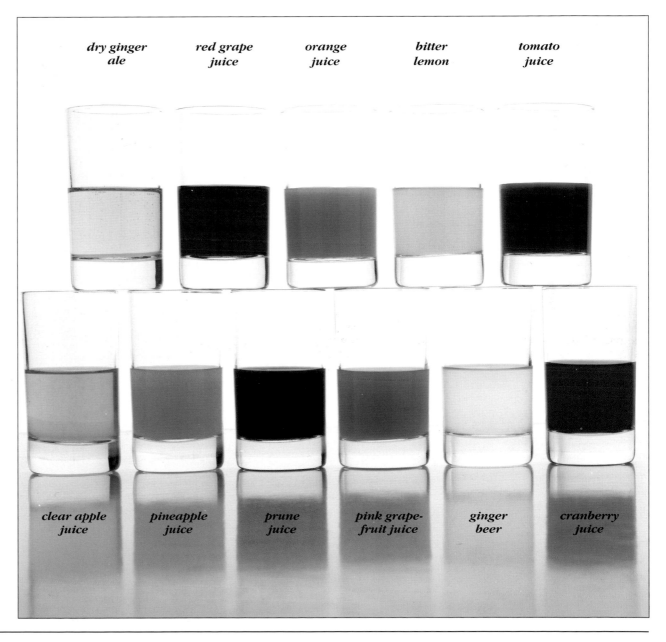

dry ginger ale   *red grape juice*   *orange juice*   *bitter lemon*   *tomato juice*

clear apple juice   *pineapple juice*   *prune juice*   *pink grapefruit juice*   *ginger beer*   *cranberry juice*

sweeter American dry. A non-alcoholic mixer, it is made from carbonated water, ginger extract and sugar. Mixes well with whiskey, bourbon and gin and is used in Kew Pimms.

Ginger Beer
A fermented drink made from ginger, sugar, water and yeast. The alcohol content in ginger beer is negligible.

Lemonade
Usually a non-alcoholic, fizzy soft drink although alcoholic varieties are now also available.

Orange Juice
For best results, either squeeze fresh oranges yourself or purchase chilled orange juice made from 100 percent fresh fruit. These have nothing added and no extra sugar. Other orange juices are mostly made with sweetened concentrates.

Passionfruit Cordial and Nectar
These are made with concentrated passionfruit juice and natural flavorings. The cordial is very strong and needs diluting to taste.

Pineapple Juice
The sweet and sour flavor of pineapple juice is imperative in many tropical cocktails. Use either freshly squeezed or out of a carton, and be sure to use the less sweet varieties.

Pink Grapefruit Juice
Often made from Florida pink grapefruits which are naturally sweet, it mixes well with white spirits. Look out for juices made from freshly squeezed fruit.

Prune Juice
This is produced in America and is made from a concentrate of dried prunes with no added sugar or preservatives.

Red Grape Juice
A light and fruity juice which is useful for making non-alcoholic cocktails. Choose cartons to keep in the cupboard and once opened, store in the fridge for no longer than three days.

Soda Water
A mixer containing sparkling water and bicarbonate of soda. Good to use when making long thirst-quenching cocktails. Sparkling mineral water or seltzer can be used in its place.

Tomato Juice
An excellent versatile mixer available in thick or thin consistencies. It can be found, mixed with clam juice, in a Canadian product called Clamato.

Tonic Water
A good old-fashioned mixer, which is used with gin, vodka or whiskey. Available in a low-calorie variety. It contains a small amount of quinine.

Added Flavors

These are the little extras that make all the difference between a good and a boring cocktail.

Bitters, Syrups and Sauces
The most widely used is angostura bitters, made in the West Indies from cloves, cinnamon, gentian, mace, nutmeg, quinine, prunes and other barks, stems and herbs. It has a distinctive flavor and rosy-red hue when a few drops are used. Grenadine and Rose's lime juice both add sweetness and hints of their own individual flavors of pomegranate and lime. Grenadine is also used for its pink/red color, which creates a glowing band at the bottom of a Mai-Tai and a Tequila Sunrise. Other herbs and spices are vital for their flavors and are used in making Tabasco sauce and Worcestershire sauce, both of which are used for maximum impact in a Bloody Mary. Balsamic and cider vinegars add a tart flavor but are less sour than lemon or lime juice.

Herbs
Ground celery seeds, fresh mint or lemon balm leaves and – during the summer months, fresh borage, chive or thyme flowers – add hints of aromatic flavors. These are used to great effect for their individual tastes and also for added color and decoration.

Spices
Freshly grated nutmeg, cloves, bruised cardamom pods, sticks of cinnamon and a pinch of cayenne, all pep up a basic punch or egg-nog; and freshly grated or creamed horseradish and fresh ginger add a zing all of their own to the simplest of juices. Use any spice with care, since an over-eager hand can easily upset the delicate balance of a cocktail. Taste the drink as you go and then add a little more if necessary.

Cocktail Equipment

To make a successful cocktail you need a few essential pieces of bartending equipment. The most vital and flamboyant is the cocktail shaker; what you have on hand in the kitchen can usually stand in for the rest. The equipment is listed below in descending order of importance.

Cocktail Shaker
Used for those drinks made with juices and syrups that need good mixing, but do not have to be crystal-clear. Cocktail shakers are usually made of stainless steel, silver, hard plastic or tough glass. The Boston shaker is made of two cup-type containers that fit over each other, one normally made of glass, the other of metal. This type is often preferred by professional bartenders. For beginners, the classic three-piece shaker is easier to handle, with its base to hold the ice and liquids, a top fitted with a built-in strainer and a tight-fitting cap.

Blender
Goblet blenders are the best shape for mixing cocktails that need to be aerated, to create a frothy cocktail or to be blended with finely crushed ice. A word of warning: do not be tempted to crush the ice in the blender, since this will blunt the blade. Opt for an ice bag or dish towel and a rolling pin and save your blender from ruin.

Ice Bag or Dish Towel
Essential for holding ice cubes when crushing, either to roughly cracked lumps or to a fine snow. The ice bag and towel must be scrupulously clean.

Wooden Hammer
For crushing the ice. The end of a wooden rolling pin also works just as well.

Short Glasses or Measuring Jug
For measuring out the required quantities. The measurements can be in single (¾ oz) or double (1½ oz) bar measures or fluid ounces. Do not switch from one type of measurement to another. 1 measure equals ¾ oz/1½ tbsp.

Strainer
Used when pouring drinks from a shaker or bar glass to a cocktail glass. The best strainers are made from stainless steel and look like a flat spoon with holes and a curl of wire on the underside. These are held over the top of the glass to keep the fruit and ice back.

Mixing Pitcher or Bar Glass
It is useful to have a container in which to mix and stir drinks that are not shaken. The glass or pitcher should be large enough to hold two or three drinks. This vessel is intended for drinks that are meant to be clear, not cloudy.

Corkscrew
The fold-away type, with a can opener and bottle opener, is the most useful to have to hand.

Bar Spoon
These long-handled spoons can reach to the bottom of the tallest tumblers and are used for mixing the drink directly in the glass. Some varieties look like a large swizzle stick with a long handle and disk at one end.

Muddler
A long stick with a bulbous end, which is used for crushing sugar or mint leaves, and so is particularly useful when creating juleps. A variety of sizes is available. They are used like a pestle in a bar glass; the smaller version is used in an individual glass.

Lemon Knife and Squeezer
Citrus fruit is essential in many cocktails; a good quality, sharp knife is required for cutting the fruit and the squeezer for extracting its juice. Although fruit juice presses are quicker to use, they are more expensive.

Nutmeg Grater
A tiny grater with small holes, for grating this hard nut over egg-nogs and frothy drinks.

Straws, Swizzle Sticks and Toothpicks
Used for the finishing decorative touches that complete a cocktail.

Zester and Canelle Knife
For presenting fruit when garnishing glasses. If you do not already have these, do not run out and buy them, since drinks can look equally attractive with simply sliced fruit.

Right: *1: blender; 2: cocktail shakers; 3: fruit juice press; 4: wooden hammer; 5: canelle knife; 6: corkscrew; 7: bar spoon; 8: strainer; 9: drinking straws; 10: shot glasses; 11: measuring spoons; 12: cup measures; 13: toothpicks; 14: swizzle sticks; 15: nutmeg grater; 16: cloth; 17: sharp knife.*

Glasses

Glasses should always be washed and dried with a glass cloth to ensure they are sparkling clean. Although some recipes suggest chilled glasses, don't put the best crystal in the freezer; leave it at the back of the refrigerator instead.

Cocktail or Martini Glass
This elegant glass is a wide conical bowl on a tall stem; a design which keeps cocktails cool by keeping warm hands away from the drink. It holds about ½ cup.

Collins Glass
The tallest of the tumblers, narrow with perfectly straight sides, it holds about 1 cup and is usually used for serving long drinks made with fresh juices or finished with soda.

Old-fashioned Glass
Classic, short whiskey tumblers are used for shorter drinks, which are served on the rocks. They hold about 6 oz.

Highball Glass
The middle-sized tumbler and the most frequently used glass. It holds about 8 oz.

Liqueur Glass
A tiny glass used to serve small measures of about 2 oz.

Brandy Balloon or Snifter
This glass is designed to trap the fragrance of the brandy in the bowl of the glass. Cupping the glass in the palms of the hands further helps to warm it gently and release its aromas.

Large Cocktail Goblets
These vary in size and shape and are used for serving larger frothy drinks, such as tropical cocktails like Piña Coladas. The wider rims of these glasses leave plenty of room for flamboyant, colorful decorations.

Champagne Glasses
Champagne can be poured into either attractive and old-fashioned champagne bowls or tall and slim flutes. The champagne flute is the more acceptable glass to use as it is more efficient at conserving the characteristic bubbles.

Red Wine Balloon
The most useful size of wine glass, holding 1 cup. It should only be filled halfway to allow the wine to be swirled around and release its bouquet.

White Wine Glass
This is a long-stemmed medium-sized glass that, once again, keeps warm hands away from the chilled wine or cocktail.

Pousse-café
A thin and narrow glass standing on a short stem. Used for floating or layered, stronger liqueur cocktails.

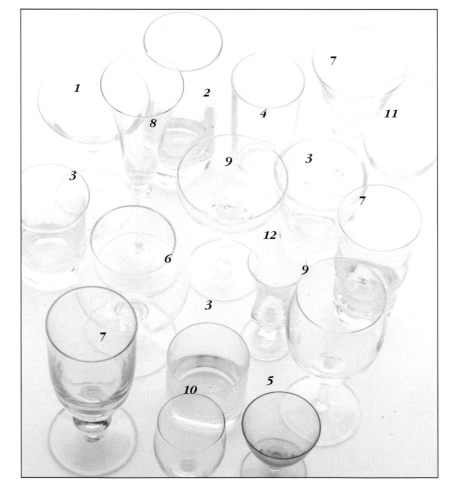

Above: *1: cocktail glass; 2: Collins glass; 3: old-fashioned glass; 4: highball glass; 5: liqueur glass; 6: brandy balloon; 7: large cocktail goblet; 8: champagne flute; 9: champagne bowl; 10: red wine balloon; 11: white wine glass; 12: pousse-café.*

Garnishes

It is far more eye-catching not to over-dress cocktails, otherwise all too quickly they turn into a fruit salad. Less is best! These edible extras add color, flavor and visual interest to any glass.

Frosting glasses with salt or sugar is a simple but effective touch, which hardly needs any extra decoration.

Edible garnishes should reflect the various contents of the cocktail. Citrus fruit is widely used because it is appetizing to look at and can be cut in advance and kept covered in the fridge, for a day, until required. Apple, pear and banana are suitable, but they do discolor on exposure to the air; dip them in lemon juice first to preserve color and flavor.

Fresh soft fruit such as strawberries, cherries, peaches, apricots and red currants make fabulous splashes of color and add a delicious flavor, but are only available in the summer.

The maraschino cherry is a popular option, and the endless supply of exotic fruits available all year long, such as mango, pineapple and star fruit, together offer numerous decorative ideas and combinations.

But not all garnishes and decorations need be fruit. Grated chocolate and nutmeg adorn egg-nogs and flips, while some Martinis call for a green olive – always opt for those packed in brine and not in oil. Plain or steeped-chili vodka can stand up to pickled chilies and the Gibson (a dry Martini) would not be a Gibson without a white pearl onion.

cherry tomatoes · apricot · nutmeg · chocolate sticks · peach · lemon · chocolate · lychees · cinnamon sticks · Cape gooseberries · chillies · mint · sugar · blackberries · sugar cubes · strawberry · orange · apple · lime · pineapple · kumquats · drinking chocolate powder · salt · black cherry · red currants · citrus rind twist · maraschino cherry · olive and pearl onion stick

Crushing Ice

Some cocktails require cracked or crushed ice for adding to glasses, or a finely crushed ice "snow" for blending. It is not a good idea to crush ice in a blender or food processor as you may find it makes the blade blunt.

Making Decorative Ice Cubes

Decorative ice cubes can instantly jazz up simple cocktails. Flavor and color the cubes with fruit juices or bitters and freeze as normal.

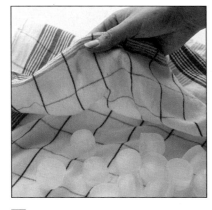

1 Lay a cloth on a work surface and cover half of the cloth with ice cubes. If you wish, you can use a cloth ice bag.

2 Fold the cloth over and, using the end of a rolling pin or a wooden mallet, strike the ice firmly several times, until you achieve the required fineness.

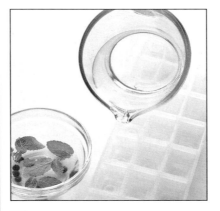

1 Fill each compartment of an ice cube tray half-full with water and place in the freezer for 2–3 hours, or until the water has frozen.

2 Prepare the fruit, olives, mint leaves, lemon rind, raisins or borage flowers and dip each briefly in water. Place in the ice-cube trays and freeze again.

3 Spoon or scrape the fine snow ice into glasses or a jug. Fine ice snow must be used immediately, but cracked or roughly crushed ice can be stored in the freezer in plastic bags.

3 Top up the ice-cube trays with water and return to the freezer to freeze completely. Use as required.

Frosting Glasses

Frosting adds both to the appearance and taste of a cocktail. Use celery salt, grated coconut, grated chocolate, colored sugars or cocoa for an eye-catching effect. Once frosted, place the glass in the fridge to chill until needed.

1 Hold the glass upside down, so the juice does not run down the glass. Rub the rim of the glass with the cut surface of a lemon, lime, orange or even a slice of fresh pineapple.

2 Keeping the glass upside down, dip the rim into a shallow layer of sugar, coconut or salt. Redip the glass, if necessary, so the rim is well-coated.

3 Stand the glass upright and let it sit until the sugar, coconut or salt has dried on the rim, then chill.

Shaking Cocktails

Cocktails that contain sugar syrups or creams require more than just a stir; they are combined and chilled with a brief shake. Remember that it is possible to shake only one or two servings at a time, so you may have to work in batches.

1 Fill the cocktail shaker two-thirds full with ice cubes and pour in the spirits; add the mixers, if not sparkling, and the flavoring ingredients.

2 Put the lid on the shaker. Hold the shaker firmly in one hand, keeping the lid in place with the other hand.

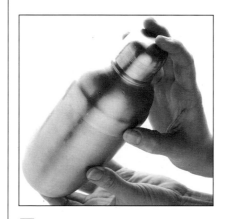

3 Shake vigorously, for about 10 seconds to blend simple concoctions and for 20–30 seconds for drinks with sugar syrups or eggs. By this time the shaker should feel cold.

4 Remove the small lid and pour into the prepared glass, using a strainer if the shaker is not already fitted with one.

Making Basic Sugar Syrup

A sugar syrup is sometimes preferable to sugar crystals for sweetening cocktails, since it immediately blends with the other ingredients.

Makes about 3 cups

INGREDIENTS
1½ cups sugar
2½ cups water

1 Place the sugar in a heavy-bottomed pan with the water, and heat gently over low heat. Stir with a wooden spoon until the sugar has dissolved.

2 Brush the sides of the pan with a pastry brush dampened in water to remove any sugar crystals that might cause the syrup to crystallize.

3 Bring to a boil for 3–5 minutes. Skim any scum and when no more appears, remove the pan from the heat.

4 Cool and pour into clean, dry, airtight bottles. Keep in the fridge for up to one month.

Making Flavored Syrup

Syrup can be flavored with anything: vanilla beans, mint or citrus peel. Just boil, then bottle with the syrup.

Makes about 1¼ cups

INGREDIENTS
2 pounds very ripe soft or stone fruit, washed
1 pound sugar

COOK'S TIP

Raspberries, black or red currants, plums and peaches all make delicious flavored syrups.

1 Place the washed fruit of your choice in a bowl and, using the bottom of a rolling pin, a wooden pestle or a potato masher, crush the fruit to release the juices. Cover and allow to sit overnight to concentrate the flavor.

2 Strain the purée through a cloth bag or piece of muslin. Gather the corners of the cloth together and twist them tight, to remove as much juice as possible. Measure the amount of juice and add 8 oz sugar to every 1¼ cups fruit juice.

3 Place the pan over low heat and gently stir until all the sugar has dissolved. Continue as in the recipe for basic sugar syrup. The syrup will keep in the fridge for up to one month.

Making Flavored Liquors

Gin, vodka and white rum can be left to steep and absorb the flavors of a wide variety of soft fruits.

Makes 4 cups

INGREDIENTS
1 pound raspberries,
  strawberries, or pineapple
1½ cups sugar
4 cups gin, vodka or light rum

VARIATIONS
Vodka and sliced bananas; white rum and fresh pineapple; gin and drained, canned lychees; sliced peaches or apricots; brandy and plums or apricots.

Steeping Spirits

Steeping any spirit with a flavoring agent, such as chilies, creates a new sensation.

Makes 4 cups

INGREDIENTS
4 cups sherry or vodka
½ cup small red chilies,
  or to taste

1 Place the fruit in a widemouth jar and add the sugar.

2 Add the liquor. Cover tightly. Leave in a cool, dark place for a month, shaking gently every week.

1 Wash and dry the chilies, discarding any that are less than perfect. Using a toothpick, prick the chilies all over to release their flavors.

2 Pack the chilies tightly into a sterilized bottle.

3 Strain through clean muslin or a cloth bag and squeeze out the rest of the liquid from the steeped fruit.

4 Return the flavored liquor to a clean bottle and seal, then store it in a cool, dark place.

3 Top up with sherry or vodka. Fit the cork tightly and leave in a dark place for at least ten days or up to two months.

VARIATIONS
Try the following interesting alternatives: gin with cumin seeds, star anise or juniper berries; brandy with ½ cup peeled and sliced fresh ginger or ⅓ cup whole cloves; vodka with ½ cup washed raisins or 1–2 tablespoons cracked black peppercorns; rum with 2–3 pricked vanilla pods. The amount of flavoring used is a matter of personal taste.

Gin Smash

Try this cocktail with any fresh mint you can find: peppermint and spearmint would each contribute their own flavor to this simple and very refreshing cocktail.

VARIATION

Use Southern Comfort or bourbon in place of the gin.

Serves 1

INGREDIENTS
1 tablespoon sugar
4 sprigs fresh mint
2 measures/3 tablespoons dry gin

gin

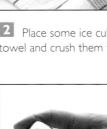

sugar

mint

1 Dissolve the sugar in a little water in the cocktail shaker.

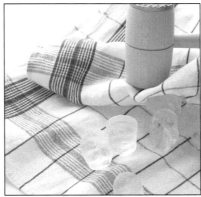

2 Place some ice cubes in a clean dish towel and crush them finely.

3 Add the mint to the cocktail shaker and, using a muddler, bruise and press the juices out of the leaves.

4 Half fill the shaker with the cracked ice and add the gin.

5 Secure the top of the shaker and shake the cocktail for about 20 seconds, to mix the gin with the mint.

6 Strain into a small wine glass filled with crushed ice. If desired, add fresh mint sprigs and drinking straws.

Gall Bracer

Short and smart, this drink is served on the rocks in a tumbler or in a long-stemmed glass with a maraschino cherry depending on the drinker and the occasion.

Serves 1

INGREDIENTS
2 dashes angostura bitters
2 dashes grenadine
2 measures/3 tablespoons whiskey
lemon rind
maraschino cherry, to decorate
   (optional)

grenadine

maraschino cherry

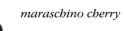
whiskey

angostura bitters

VARIATION

For a longer drink, finish with soda or sparkling mineral water, or for a cocktail called a Gall Trembler, substitute gin for the whiskey and add more bitters.

1 Half fill a bar glass with ice cubes. Add the angostura bitters, grenadine and whiskey and stir well to chill.

2 Place some ice in a short tumbler and pour the cocktail over it.

3 Holding the lemon rind between your fingers, squeeze out the oil and juices into the cocktail. Discard the lemon rind.

4 Decorate with a cherry, if desired.

Gibson

Well loved in Japan, this is a version of the Martini with a pearl onion, rather than the usual twist of lemon. You may prefer to use a higher proportion of gin.

Serves 1

INGREDIENTS
$^1/_2$ measure/2 teaspoons extra-dry
    vermouth
1 scant measure/$1^1/_4$ tablespoons
    extra-dry gin
2 pearl onions, to decorate

extra-dry vermouth

gin

pearl onions

VARIATION

Add a touch more dry vermouth and a twist of lemon and you have an Australian Kangaroo.

1 Pour the vermouth into a bar glass of ice, stir briskly and then pour out the liquid. Only the vermouth that clings to the ice and glass should be used.

2 Add the gin and stir for at least 30 seconds to chill well.

3 Strain into a martini glass, either on the rocks or straight up.

4 Thread the pearl onions onto a toothpick and add to the drink.

Brandy Alexander

A warming digestif, made from a blend of crème de cacao, brandy and double cream, that can be served at the end of the meal with coffee.

Serves 1

INGREDIENTS
1 measure/1$^{1}/_{2}$ tablespoons
   brandy
1 measure/1$^{1}/_{2}$ tablespoons
   crème de cacao
1 measure/1$^{1}/_{2}$ tablespoons
   heavy cream
whole nutmeg,
   to decorate

crème de cacao

nutmeg

heavy cream

brandy

VARIATION

Warm the brandy and the heavy cream gently and add to a blender with the crème de cacao. Blend until frothy. Serve with a cinnamon stick.

1 Half fill the cocktail shaker with ice and pour in the brandy, crème de cacao and the cream.

2 Shake for about 20 seconds to mix thoroughly.

3 Strain the chilled cocktail into a small wine glass.

4 Finely grate a little nutmeg over the top of the cocktail.

Perfect Manhattan

When making Manhattans it's a matter of preference whether you use sweet vermouth, dry vermouth or a mixture of the two. Both of the former require a dash of angostura bitters.

Serves 1

INGREDIENTS
2 measures/3 tablespoons rye
    whiskey
¼ measure/1 teaspoon dry
    vermouth
¼ measure/1 teaspoon sweet
    vermouth
1 lemon
maraschino cherry,
    to decorate

sweet vermouth

maraschino cherry

whiskey

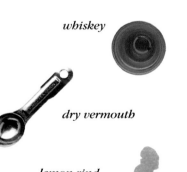

dry vermouth

lemon rind

VARIATION

Create a Skyscraper by adding a dash of angostura bitters, a teaspoon of maraschino cherry juice, and finish with ginger ale.

1 Pour the whiskey and vermouths into a bar glass half full of ice. Stir well for 30 seconds to mix and chill.

2 Strain on the rocks or straight up into a chilled cocktail glass.

3 Using a canelle knife, pare away a small strip of lemon rind. Tie it into a knot to help release the oils from the rind, and drop it into the cocktail.

4 To finish, add a maraschino cherry with its stalk left intact.

Margarita

Traditionally, this popular strong apéritif is made with tequila and Cointreau, but it is also good made with vodka and triple sec (an orange-flavored liqueur similar to white curaçao).

VARIATION
Replace the Cointreau with blue curaçao for a vivid color and a stimulating flavor.

Serves 1

INGREDIENTS
1 measure/1¹/₂ tablespoons
    tequila
1 measure/1¹/₂ tablespoons
    Cointreau
²/₃ measure/1 tablespoon fresh lime
    juice
wedge of fresh lime, fine salt
    and cucumber, to decorate

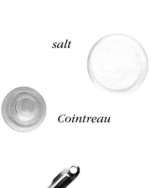

tequila

salt

Cointreau

lime juice

cucumber peel

1 Rub the rim of the glass with a wedge of fresh lime.

2 Invert the glass into fine salt to create a rim of salt. Turn the glass the right way up and chill until required.

3 Pour the tequila and Cointreau, with the lime juice, into a cocktail shaker filled with ice. Shake for 20 seconds.

4 Carefully strain the cocktail into the frosted glass.

5 Using a sharp knife or vegetable peeler, cut a long thin strip of green peel from a whole cucumber.

6 Trim the cucumber peel to size and thread it onto a toothpick. Add to the glass to decorate.

Hooded Claw

Syrupy-sweet prune juice with Amaretto and Cointreau makes a delicious digestif when poured over finely crushed ice snow.

Serves 4

INGREDIENTS
5 measures/½ cup prune
   juice
2 measures/3 tablespoons
   Amaretto
1 measure/1½ tablespoons
   Cointreau

Amaretto

Cointreau

prune juice

1 Pour the prune juice, Amaretto and Cointreau into a cocktail shaker half filled with ice.

2 Shake the cocktail for 20 seconds to chill well.

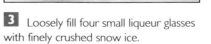

3 Loosely fill four small liqueur glasses with finely crushed snow ice.

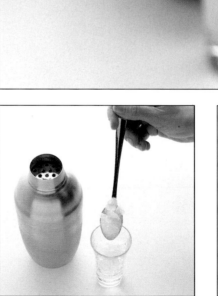

4 Strain the drink into the glasses and serve with short straws.

Bitter Gimlet

An old-fashioned apéritif, which could easily be turned into a longer drink by finishing it with chilled tonic or soda water.

Serves 1

INGREDIENTS
1 lime, cut into wedges
1 measure/1¹/₂ tablespoons gin
2 dashes angostura bitters
slice and rind of lime, to decorate

lime wedges

lime decoration

angostura bitters

gin

VARIATION
Add a teaspoon of sugar, for a sweeter version, or a dash or two of crème de menthe to create a Fallen Angel.

1 Place the lime at the bottom of the bar glass and, using a muddler, press the juice out of the lime.

2 Add cracked ice, the gin and the bitters and stir well until chilled.

3 Strain the cocktail into a short tumbler over ice cubes.

4 Add a triangle of lime rind to the drink and rest a slice of lime on the rim of the glass.

Chili Vodkatini

Not quite a Martini, but almost. Over the years, the proportions of vodka to vermouth have varied widely, with the vodka becoming almost overwhelming. Be sure to have your chili vodka made well in advance and ready to use.

VARIATION

For the classic Martini, use gin, but serve with a twist of lemon. Mix plain vodka and dry vermouth for a Vodka Martini. Add an olive and it becomes a Vodka Gibson.

Serves 1

INGREDIENTS

1 measure/$1\frac{1}{2}$ tablespoons chili vodka

$\frac{1}{4}$ measure/1 teaspoon medium or dry French vermouth

2 small pickled or vodka-soaked chilies, to decorate

1 pitted green olive, to decorate

chili vodka

dry vermouth

chili-stuffed olive

1 Add the chili vodka to a bar glass of ice and mix for about 30 seconds, until the outside of the glass is frosted over.

2 Add the vermouth to a chilled cocktail glass and swirl it around the inside of the glass to wet it. Discard any remaining vermouth.

3 Cut one of the pickled chilies in half and discard the seeds. Stuff the pitted green olive with the chili.

4 Thread the stuffed olive onto a toothpick with the remaining chili.

5 Strain the cocktail into the prepared cocktail glass.

6 Add the olive and chili decoration to the drink before serving.

Gin Crusta

Prepare the glass in advance and keep it chilled in the fridge ready for instant use! The depth of pink color will depend on the strength of the maraschino cherry juice you use.

VARIATION
Make in the same way with whiskey, Southern Comfort, brandy or rum.

Serves 1

INGREDIENTS
1 lemon
3 dashes sugar syrup
2 dashes maraschino cherry juice
2 dashes angostura bitters
1 measure/1½ tablespoons dry gin
2 tablespoons golden granulated sugar

angostura bitters

maraschino cherry juice

golden granulated sugar

lemon juice

gin

sugar syrup

lemon rind

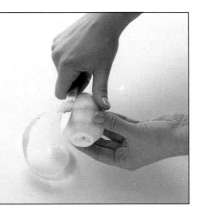

1 Cut both ends off the lemon and, using a paring knife or canelle knife, peel the lemon thinly, as you would an apple, in one long, continuous piece.

2 Halve the whole lemon and rub the edge of a glass with one half.

3 Turn the glass upside-down and dip it into the granulated sugar to create a decorative rim.

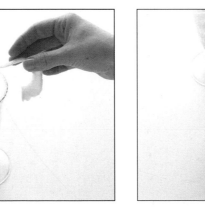

4 Arrange the lemon rind in a scroll on the inside of the glass.

5 Add the sugar syrup, maraschino cherry juice, angostura bitters, gin and juice of ¼ of the lemon to a cocktail shaker, half filled with ice.

6 Shake for about 30 seconds and carefully strain into the prepared glass.

Airstrike

A variation on a Val d'Isère Shooter, similar to the Italian Flaming Sambuca.

Serves 1

INGREDIENTS
2 measures/3 tablespoons Galliano
1 measure/1½ tablespoons brandy
1 star anise

Galliano

star anise

brandy

VARIATION
Use only Sambuca and float two or three fresh coffee beans on the surface instead of the star anise before lighting.

1 Put the Galliano and brandy in a small saucepan and heat very gently, until just warm.

2 Carefully pour into a heat-resistant glass standing on a small plate or saucer; add the star anise.

3 Using a lighted taper or long match, pass the flame over the surface of the drink to ignite it. The flame will be low and very pale, so be careful not to burn yourself.

4 Let burn for a couple of minutes, until the star anise has sizzled a little and released its aroma into the drink. Cool slightly before drinking. Beware, the top of the glass will be hot!

B-52

This cocktail depends on the difference in specific weight or densities of each of the liqueurs to remain strictly separated in layers.

Serves 1

INGREDIENTS
1 measure/1$\frac{1}{2}$ tablespoons Kahlúa
1 measure/1$\frac{1}{2}$ tablespoons
  Grand Marnier
1 measure/1$\frac{1}{2}$ tablespoons
  Bailey's Irish Cream

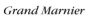

Grand Marnier

Bailey's Irish Cream

Kahlúa

VARIATION

Create a similar effect with equal quantities of Bailey's, Kahlúa and vodka, layered in that order. Or try Chartreuse, cherry brandy and kümmel with cumin seeds floated on the top instead.

1 Pour the Kahlúa into a small shot glass or pousse-café.

2 Hold a cold teaspoon upside-down, just barely touching the surface of the Kahlúa and the side of the glass.

3 Slowly and carefully pour the Grand Marnier over the back of the teaspoon to create a second layer.

4 In the same way, carefully pour the Bailey's over the back of a second clean teaspoon to create a final layer. This layer in fact will form the middle layer and push the Grand Marnier to the top.

Coffee and Chocolate Flip

Since the egg is not cooked, use only the freshest eggs. For a hint of honey, substitute Drambuie for the brandy, but omit the sugar. Replace the Kahlúa with Tia Maria for a less sweet version.

VARIATION
Shake together equal quantities of Kahlúa, chocolate-flavored milk and coffee. Serve on the rocks.

Serves 1

INGREDIENTS
1 egg
1 tsp sugar
1 measure/1$\frac{1}{2}$ tablespoons brandy
1 measure/1$\frac{1}{2}$ tablespoons Kahlúa
1 tsp instant coffee granules
3 measures/4$\frac{1}{2}$ tablespoons heavy
   cream
cocoa powder or grated
   chocolate, to decorate

instant coffee granules

egg

sugar

cocoa powder

heavy cream   Kahlúa

brandy

1 Separate the egg and lightly beat the white until frothy and white.

2 In a separate bowl, beat the egg yolk with the sugar.

3 In a small saucepan, combine the brandy, Kahlúa, coffee and cream and warm over very low heat.

4 Allow the mixture to cool, then whisk it into the egg yolk.

5 Add the egg white to the egg and cream and pour the mixture briefly back and forth between two glasses, until it is smooth.

6 Pour into a tall glass over coarsely crushed ice and sprinkle the top with cocoa powder.

Cranberry Kiss

A delicious full-flavored cocktail with the tang of cranberry and pink grapefruit juices and the sweetness of Marsala.

Serves 1

INGREDIENTS
2 measures/3 tablespoons cranberry
    juice
1 measure/1½ tablespoons
    brandy
2 measures/3 tablespoons pink
    grapefruit juice
2 measures/3 tablespoons Marsala
red currants, to decorate
1 egg white, lightly beaten, and
    1 tablespoon sugar, to decorate

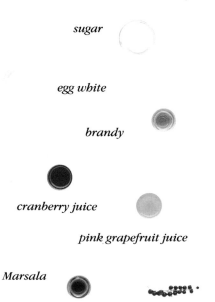

sugar

egg white

brandy

cranberry juice

pink grapefruit juice

Marsala

red currants

1 For the decoration, lightly brush the red currants with the egg white.

2 Shake sugar over the red currants, to cover with a frosting. Set aside to dry.

3 Add the cranberry juice, brandy and grapefruit juice to a cocktail shaker full of crushed ice and shake for 20 seconds.

4 Strain into a well chilled glass.

5 Tilt the glass slightly before slowly pouring in the Marsala down the side of the glass.

6 Serve, decorated with the frosted red currants.

Grasshopper

A minted, creamy cocktail in an attractive shade of green. If you use dark crème de cacao, the cocktail will not be as vibrant a color, but you'll find that it tastes just as good.

Serves 1

INGREDIENTS
2 measures/3 tablespoons crème de menthe
2 measures/3 tablespoons light crème de cacao
2 measures/3 tablespoons heavy cream
melted bittersweet chocolate, to decorate

heavy cream

crème de menthe

crème de cacao

bittersweet chocolate

1 Pour the crème de menthe and crème de cacao into a cocktail shaker and add the cream.

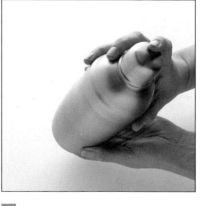

2 Add some cracked ice and shake well for 20 seconds.

3 Strain the cocktail into a tumbler of finely cracked ice.

4 To decorate, spread the melted chocolate evenly over a plastic board and leave to cool and harden. Draw the blade of a sharp knife across the chocolate to create curls. Add to the top of the cocktail.

VARIATION

Mix in a blender with crushed ice for a smoother consistency. To make a Scandinavian Freeze, mix 2 measures each of vodka and crème de cacao and a scoop of vanilla ice cream and process until just smooth.

Tequila Sunset

This variation on the popular party drink can be mixed and chilled in a pitcher, ready to pour into glasses, and finished at the last minute with the addition of crème de cassis and honey.

Serves 1

INGREDIENTS
1 measure/1^1/$_2$ tablespoons clear or golden tequila
5 measures/^{1}/$_2$ cup fresh lemon juice, chilled
1 measure/1^1/$_2$ tablespoons orange juice, chilled
1–2 tablespoons clear honey
^{2}/$_3$ measure/1 tablespoon crème de cassis

crème de cassis

lemon juice

tequila

orange juice

honey

VARIATION

To make a Tequila Sunrise, mix 2 parts tequila with 6 parts orange juice and 2 parts grenadine, then stir gently together.

1 Pour the tequila and the lemon and orange juices into a well-chilled cocktail glass.

2 Using a swizzle stick, mix the ingredients by twisting the stick between the palms of your hands.

3 Drizzle the honey into the center of the cocktail. It will sink and create a layer at the bottom of the glass.

4 Add the crème de cassis, but do not stir. It will create a glowing layer above the honey at the bottom of the glass.

Vunderful

A long, lazy Sunday afternoon tipple, conjured up in the heat of Zimbabwe. Leave the fruits in the gin for as long as possible.

VARIATION
Use fresh apricots or nectarines and finish either with ginger beer or ginger ale.

Serves 20

INGREDIENTS
14-ounce can lychees
2 peaches, sliced
2½ cups gin

For each serving you will need:
1 measure/1½ tablespoons Pimms
2–3 dashes bitters
5 measures/½ cup chilled
    tonic water or lemonade
slices of lime, to decorate

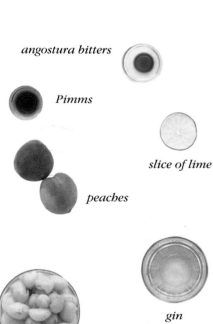

angostura bitters

Pimms

slice of lime

peaches

gin

lychees

lemonade

1 Strain the lychees from the syrup and place them in a widemouth jar with the peach slices and the gin. Let sit overnight or up to a month.

2 In a large bar glass or jug, mix for each serving 1 measure/1½ tbsp of the lychee gin with the Pimms and the bitters to taste.

3 Strain into tall tumblers filled with ice cubes.

4 Add chilled tonic water or lemonade to taste.

5 Put some of the drained gin-soaked lychees and peaches into each glass and stir and crush the fruit into the drink using a muddler.

6 Add half a slice of lime to the rim of each glass and serve.

Blue Hawaiian

This drink can be decorated as flamboyantly as Carmen Miranda's headdress with a mixture of fruits and leaves – an eye-catching colorful cocktail that you'll find very drinkable.

VARIATION

Pour equal quantities of vodka and blue curaçao over ice. Finish with lemonade for a Blue Lagoon or add equal amounts of gin and curaçao, plus angostura bitters for a Blue Cloak.

Serves 1

INGREDIENTS
1 measure/1½ tablespoons blue curaçao
1 measure/1½ tablespoons coconut cream
2 measures/3 tablespoons light rum
2 measures/3 tablespoons pineapple juice
leaves and wedge of pineapple, slice of prickly pear or orange, a wedge of lime and a maraschino cherry, to decorate

1 Put the curaçao, coconut cream and light rum in a blender. Process very briefly until the color is even.

2 Place ice cubes between a dish towel and crush to a fine snow with a wooden hammer or rolling pin.

3 Add the pineapple juice to the blender and process the mixture once more until frothy.

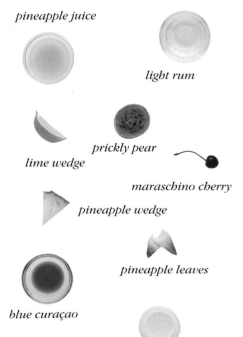

pineapple juice

light rum

prickly pear

lime wedge

maraschino cherry

pineapple wedge

pineapple leaves

blue curaçao

coconut cream

4 Spoon the crushed ice into a large cocktail glass or goblet.

5 Pour the cocktail from the blender over the crushed ice.

6 Decorate with the pineapple leaves and wedge, prickly pear or orange slice, a lime wedge and a maraschino cherry. Serve with a couple of drinking straws.

Mai Tai

A very refreshing but strong party drink that slides down easily; just before you do!

Serves 1

INGREDIENTS

1 measure/1½ tablespoons
   light rum
1 measure/1½ tablespoons dark
   rum
1 measure/1½ tablespoons
   apricot brandy
3 measures/4½ tablespoons
   orange juice, chilled
3 measures/4½ tablespoons
   pineapple juice, chilled
1 measure/1½ tablespoons
   grenadine

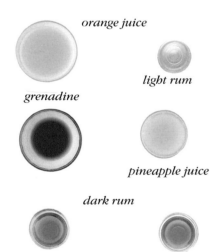

orange juice

light rum

grenadine

pineapple juice

dark rum

apricot brandy

VARIATION

Mix bitters, rum and orgeat (almond and orange flower water) syrup or almond essence into 1½ cups orange juice.

1 Add the light and dark rum and apricot brandy to a cocktail shaker half full of cracked ice.

2 Add the well-chilled orange and pineapple juices.

3 Shake well for about 20 seconds, or until the cocktail shaker feels cold. Strain into a tumbler of ice.

4 Slowly pour the grenadine into the glass and it will sink to the bottom of the drink to make a glowing red layer.

Morning Glory Fizz

A good early-morning drink, which should be consumed as soon as it is made, before it loses its flavor and bubbles.

Serves 1

INGREDIENTS

$^2/_3$ measure/1 tablespoon brandy
$^1/_4$ measure/1 teaspoon orange curaçao
$^1/_4$ measure/1 teaspoon fresh lemon juice
1 dash anisette
2 dashes angostura bitters
soda water, to taste
twist of lemon rind, to decorate

anisette

orange curaçao

brandy

angostura bitters

lemon juice

soda water

lemon rind

1 Pour the brandy, curaçao, lemon juice and anisette into a cocktail shaker containing ice and shake for 20 seconds.

2 Strain the drink into a small chilled cocktail glass.

3 Add the angostura bitters to taste and finish with the soda water.

4 Using a canelle knife, cut a long thin piece of lemon rind. Curl the lemon rind into a tight coil and add to the drink.

VARIATION

Shake together an egg white, sugar syrup to taste, the juice of $^1/_2$ lemon and $^1/_2$ lime and gin or whiskey instead of the brandy, then add a splash of Chartreuse. Shake well and finish with soda.

Cider Cup

Cups make an excellent long and refreshing drink for
an apéritif or party. Mix up just before serving.

Serves 6

INGREDIENTS
rind of 1 lemon
slices of orange
5 measures/½ cup pale
    sherry
3 measures/4½ tablespoons brandy
    or clove brandy
3 measures/4½ tablespoons white
    curaçao
2 measures/3 tablespoons amaretto
2½ cups good quality
    hard cider
cucumber, to decorate

cucumber peel

orange slices

amaretto

lemon rind

pale sherry

hard cider

white curaçao

brandy

1 Partially fill a pitcher with cracked
ice and stir in the lemon rind and the
orange slices.

2 Add the sherry, brandy, curaçao and
amaretto to the ice and stir well to mix.

3 Pour in the cider and stir gently with
a long swizzle stick.

4 Using a canelle knife, peel the
cucumber around in a continuous piece,
to produce a spiral. Serve the cocktail in
chilled glasses, decorated with the fruit
and a twist of cucumber peel.

VARIATION

Instead of brandy, use Calvados for
a richer flavor and add a little
maraschino cherry juice to give
more color.

Havana Cobbler

An old-fashioned drink that is surprisingly refreshing served in hot weather.

Serves 1

INGREDIENTS
1 tsp sugar syrup
$^1/_2$ measure/2 teaspoons green
   ginger wine
1 measure/1$^1/_2$ tablespoons
   Cuban or light rum
1 measure/1$^1/_2$ tablespoons port

light rum

sugar syrup

 ginger wine

port

VARIATION

Cobblers can be made with brandy, gin and sherry and even wine or champagne; obviously if you use the latter, remember not to shake it! And omit the port!

1 Put the sugar syrup and ginger wine in a cocktail shaker half filled with ice. Add the light rum.

2 Shake together for 20 seconds.

3 Strain the cocktail into a chilled short tumbler.

4 Tilt the glass and slowly pour the port down the side of the glass to form a floating layer on top of the cocktail.

Moscow Mule

One of the classic American vodka-based cocktails, which uses a large quantity of angostura bitters for its flavor and color and enough vodka to give the drink a real kick.

Serves 1

INGREDIENTS
2 measures/3 tablespoons vodka
6 dashes angostura bitters
dash of Rose's lime juice
$^1/_2$ measure/2 teaspoons fresh lime juice
3 measures/$4^1/_2$ tablespoons ginger beer
slices of lime, to decorate

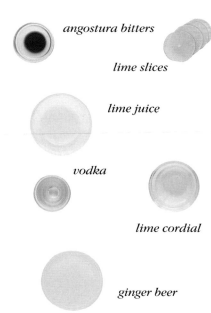

angostura bitters

lime slices

lime juice

vodka

lime cordial

ginger beer

1 Pour the vodka, bitters, lime cordial and lime juice into a bar glass of ice. Mix together well with a bar spoon.

2 Strain into a tumbler containing a couple of ice cubes.

3 Finish the mixture to taste with ginger beer.

4 Add a few halved slices of lime to the cocktail before serving.

VARIATION

For a Malawi Shandy, mix ice-cold ginger beer with a dash of bitters and finish with soda water. Of course, the vodka does not have to be left out.

Vodka and Kumquat Lemonade

A mild-sounding name for a strong concoction of kumquat and peppercorn-flavoured vodka and white curaçao.

VARIATION
Use fruit cordial, with gin or vodka as the base, and finish with soda or tonic water.

Serves 2

INGREDIENTS
3 ounces kumquats
5 measures/½ cup vodka
3 black peppercorns, cracked (optional)
²/₃ measure/1 tablespoon white curaçao or orange syrup
²/₃ measure/1 tablespoon lemon juice
7 measures/ ²/₃ cup sparkling mineral or soda water
slices of kumquats and fresh mint sprigs, to decorate

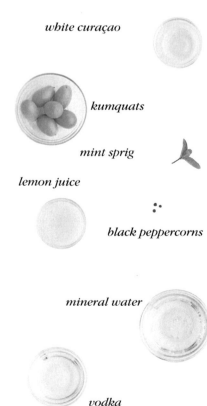

white curaçao

kumquats

mint sprig

lemon juice

black peppercorns

mineral water

vodka

1 Thickly slice the kumquats and add to the vodka in an airtight jar with the cracked black peppercorns, if using. Set aside for a couple of hours, overnight or for up to a month.

2 Fill a pitcher with cracked ice and then add the curaçao or orange syrup, the lemon juice and the kumquat-flavored vodka with the sliced kumquats.

3 Using a long swizzle stick, stir together well.

4 Add the mineral or soda water and a few fresh mint leaves and gently stir everything together.

5 Pour the drink into chilled glasses of ice.

6 Add slices of kumquats to the glasses and decorate with more mint sprigs.

Horse's Fall

A long drink to serve on a hot summer's day. The addition of strongly flavored tea is a matter of taste and preference.

VARIATION
Substitute Calvados or brandy for the flavored tea for a Horse's Neck.

Serves 1

INGREDIENTS
1 lemon
dash angostura bitters
2 measures/3 tablespoons raspberry, Orange Pekoe or Assam tea, chilled (optional)
1 measure/1½ tablespoons unsweetened apple juice
5 measures/about ½ cup dry ginger ale or lemonade

apple juice

lemon rind

angostura bitters

raspberry tea

dry ginger ale

1 Cut the peel from the lemon in one continuous strip and use it to line and decorate a long cocktail glass. Chill the glass until needed.

2 Add a dash of angostura bitters to the bottom of the glass.

3 Measure the tea, if using, into the cocktail shaker and add the apple juice.

4 Shake everything together for about 20 seconds.

5 Strain into the prepared chilled cocktail glass.

6 Finish with chilled ginger ale or lemonade to taste.

Sunburst

Bursting with freshness and vitamins, this drink is a good early morning pick-me-up.

Serves 2

INGREDIENTS
1 green apple, cored and
   chopped
3 carrots, peeled and chopped
1 mango, peeled, and pitted
7 measures/⅔ cup freshly
   squeezed orange juice, chilled
6 strawberries, hulled
slice of orange, to decorate

mango

orange juice

orange slice

carrots

green apple

strawberries

1 Place the apple, carrots and mango in a blender or food processor and process to a pulp.

2 Add the orange juice and strawberries and process again.

3 Strain well through a sieve, pressing out all the juice with the back of a wooden spoon. Discard any pulp left in the sieve.

4 Pour into tumblers filled with ice cubes and serve immediately, decorated with a slice of orange.

VARIATION

Any combination of fruit juice and yogurt can be shaken together. Try natural yogurt with apple, apricot and mango.

Scarlet Lady

This drink could fool a few on the first sip, with its fruity and fresh tones. It could easily pass as an alcoholic wine-based cocktail.

Serves 1

INGREDIENTS

¼ pound cubed Galia, honeydew or
   watermelon
5 small red seedless grapes
3 measures/4½ tablespoons
   unsweetened red grape juice
red seedless grapes, sugar-frosted,
   1 egg white, lightly beaten and
   1 tablespoon sugar, to decorate

red grape juice

egg white

melon

sugar

red grapes

VARIATION

For a longer fizzy drink, finish the melon and grape purée with equal quantities of grape juice and tonic or soda water.

1 Put the melon and grapes in a blender and process until they form a smooth purée.

2 Add the red grape juice and continue to process for another minute.

3 Strain the juice into a bar glass of ice and stir until chilled.

4 Pour into a chilled cocktail glass and decorate with sugar-frosted grapes threaded onto a toothpick.

Virgin Prairie Oyster

A superior pick-me-up and a variation on the Bloody Mary. The tomato base can be drunk without the raw egg yolk if it does not appeal to you. Use only fresh free-range eggs.

Serves 1

INGREDIENTS
¾ cup tomato juice
2 teaspoons Worcestershire sauce
1–2 teaspoons balsamic vinegar
1 egg yolk
cayenne pepper, to taste

balsamic vinegar

tomato juice

egg yolk

Worcestershire sauce

cayenne pepper

VARIATION

Shake together equal quantities of fresh grapefruit juice and tomato juice with a dash of Worcestershire sauce. Strain into a tall and narrow highball glass.

1 Measure the tomato juice into a large bar glass and stir over plenty of ice until well chilled.

2 Strain into a tall tumbler half filled with ice cubes.

3 Add the Worcestershire sauce and balsamic vinegar to taste and mix with a swizzle stick.

4 Float the egg yolk on top and lightly dust with cayenne pepper.

Fruit and Ginger Ale

An old English mulled drink, served chilled over ice. Of course it can be made with ready-squeezed apple and orange juices, but roasting the fruit with cloves gives a much better flavor.

Serves 4–6

INGREDIENTS
1 cooking apple
1 orange, scrubbed
1 lemon, scrubbed
20 whole cloves
3-inch piece fresh ginger, peeled
1 ounce light brown sugar
1½ cups bitter lemon or non-alcoholic wine
wedges of orange rind and whole cloves, to decorate

ginger

light brown sugar

orange *bitter lemon*

whole cloves

lemon

orange rind *cooking apple*

1 Preheat the oven to 400°F. Score the apple around the middle and stud the orange and lemon with the cloves. Bake the fruits in the oven for about 25 minutes, until soft and completely cooked through.

2 Quarter the orange and lemon, mash the apple, discarding the peel and the core. Finely grate the ginger. Place the fruit and ginger in a bowl with the light brown sugar.

3 Add 1¼ cups boiling water. Using a spoon, squeeze the fruit to release more flavor. Cover and let sit for an hour or overnight until cool.

4 Strain into a jug of cracked ice and use a spoon to press out all the juices from the fruit. Add the bitter lemon or non-alcoholic wine to taste. Decorate with orange rind and cloves.

Blushing Piña Colada

This is good with or without the rum. Don't be tempted to put roughly crushed ice into the blender; it will not be as smooth and will ruin the blades. Make sure you crush it well first.

VARIATION

For a classic Piña Colada, use vanilla ice cream and 1 measure light rum. For a Passionate Encounter, blend 2 scoops passionfruit sorbet and coconut milk with a measure each of pineapple and apricot juice.

Serves 2

INGREDIENTS
1 banana, peeled and sliced
1 thick slice pineapple, peeled
3 measures/4¹/₂ tablespoons
   pineapple juice
1 scoop strawberry ice cream or
   sorbet
1 measure/1¹/₂ tablespoons
   unsweetened coconut milk
2 tablespoons grenadine
pineapple wedges and
   maraschino cherries, to decorate

coconut milk

pineapple slice

pineapple juice

grenadine

maraschino cherry

strawberry ice cream

banana

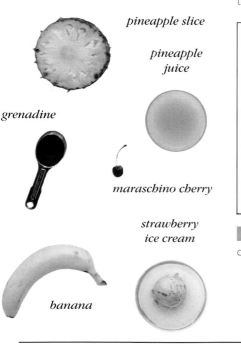

1 Roughly chop the banana. Cut two small wedges from the pineapple for decoration and set aside. Cut up the remainder of the pineapple and add it to the blender with the banana.

2 Add the pineapple juice to the blender and process until the mixture is a smooth purée.

3 Add the strawberry ice cream or sorbet with the coconut milk and a small scoop of finely crushed ice, and process until smooth.

4 Pour into two large, well-chilled cocktail glasses.

5 Pour the grenadine syrup slowly on top of the drink; it will filter down creating a dappled effect.

6 Decorate each glass with a wedge of pineapple and a cherry and serve with drinking straws.

Volunteer

This drink is ideal for a lazy summer afternoon. It's also a fine cocktail to serve the designated driver at a party. It was devised and drunk during a very rough channel crossing in too small a boat!

Serves 1

INGREDIENTS
2 measures/3 tablespoons lime
  cordial
2– 3 dashes angostura bitters
7 measures/²⁄₃ cup chilled
  tonic water
decorative ice cubes, to serve
frozen slices of lime, to decorate

tonic water

angostura bitters

lime cordial

frozen lime slice

1 Place the lime cordial at the bottom of the glass and shake in the angostura bitters to taste.

2 Add a few decorative ice cubes to the glass, if liked.

3 Finish with tonic water and add the frozen lime slices.

VARIATION

Use fresh lime or grapefruit juice and a splash of sugar syrup instead of the lime cordial, and finish with ginger ale.

Steel Works

A thirst quenching drink, which is ideal to serve at any time of the day.

Serves 1

INGREDIENTS
2 measures/3 tablespoons
    passionfruit cordial
dash angostura bitters
3 measures/4½ tablespoons soda
    water, chilled
3 measures/4½ tablespoons
    lemonade, chilled
1 passionfruit (optional)

lemonade

passionfruit cordial

passionfruit

soda water

angostura bitters

1 Pour the passionfruit cordial straight into a long tumbler. Add the angostura bitters to the glass and then add some ice cubes.

2 Finish the drink with the chilled soda water and lemonade and stir briefly together.

3 Cut the passionfruit in half, if using; scoop the seeds and flesh from the fruit and add to the drink. Stir the drink gently before serving.

VARIATION

For a Rock Shandy, pour equal parts of lemonade and soda over bitters or use your favorite variety of the naturally flavored and unsweetened fruit cordials.

Bandrek

A rich and creamy version of the spicy Indonesian drink. Serve warm or chilled. If you like, add a very fresh egg to the syrup and mix in the blender, and you'll have an egg-nog.

VARIATION

Stir $^1\!/_2$ measure/2 teaspoons whiskey into the finished drink or add the strained spiced syrup to double-strength black coffee. Process in a blender with a little heavy cream, strain and serve over ice.

Serves 1

INGREDIENTS
3 whole cloves
3 juniper berries, bruised
1 cinnamon stick
6 green cardamom pods, bruised
4 whole black peppercorns
1 sugar cube
$^3\!/_4$ cup water
2 measures/3 tablespoons unsweetened coconut milk
3 measures/$4^1\!/_2$ tablespoons whole milk
cinnamon sticks and a maraschino cherry, to decorate

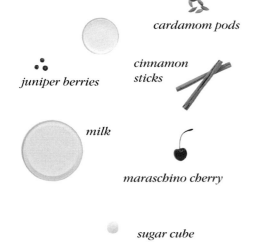

coconut milk

cardamom pods

cinnamon sticks

juniper berries

milk

maraschino cherry

sugar cube

1 Put the cloves, juniper berries, cinnamon, cardamom pods, peppercorns and sugar cube in a saucepan. Heat gently to release the aromas and flavors of the spices.

2 Add the water and bring to the boil over medium-high heat.

3 Continue to boil for 10 minutes or until reduced to 2–3 tablespoons of spicy flavored syrup. Remove from the heat and cool.

4 Pour the syrup into a blender with the coconut milk and whole milk and process until smooth.

5 Strain over cracked ice into a stemmed glass.

6 Decorate with cinnamon sticks and a maraschino cherry.

St. Clements

Oranges and lemons create a simple but thirst-quenching drink, which confirms that freshly squeezed fruit has a superior flavor to any of the ready-squeezed versions you can buy.

VARIATION

This same principle can be used to make pineapple, peach, grape and soft fruit juices, but sweeten with sugar syrup. These infusions will keep in the fridge for 2–3 days.

Serves 1

INGREDIENTS
2 oranges
1 lemon
$^1/_2$ ounce sugar, or to taste
5 tablespoons water
orange and lemon slices, to
    decorate

oranges

sugar

lemon

*orange and
lemon slices*

1 Wash the oranges and lemons and then pare the rind off the fruit with a sharp knife, leaving the white pith behind. Remove the pith from the fruit and discard it.

2 Put the orange and lemon rind in a saucepan with the sugar and water. Place over low heat and stir gently until the sugar has dissolved.

3 Remove the pan from the heat and press the orange and lemon rind against the sides of the pan to release all their oils. Cover the pan and let cool. Remove and discard the rind.

4 Purée the oranges and lemon and sweeten the fruit pulp by pouring the cooled citrus syrup over the fruit pulp. Set aside for 2–3 hours to allow the flavors to infuse.

5 Strain the fruit pulp, pressing the solids in the sieve to extract as much of the juice as possible.

6 Pour into a tall glass filled with finely crushed ice and decorate with a slice of orange and lemon.

Dickson's Bloody Mary

This recipe has plenty of character with horseradish, sherry and Tabasco. The true Bloody Mary is simpler.

VARIATION
Use tequila in place of the vodka for a Bloody Maria, use a clam juice and tomato juice mixture for a Bloody Muddle.

Serves 1

INGREDIENTS
2 measures/3 tablespoons vodka or
  chili-flavoured vodka
1 measure/1¹/₂ tablespoons
  fino sherry
7 measures/²/₃ cup
  tomato juice
1 measure/1¹/₂ tablespoons
  lemon juice
2–3 dashes Tabasco sauce
2–3 teaspoons Worcestershire
  sauce
¹/₂ teaspoon creamed horseradish
1 teaspoon celery salt
salt and ground black pepper
celery stalk, stuffed green olives and a
  cherry tomato, to decorate

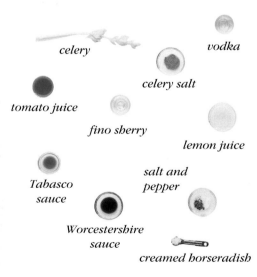

celery

vodka

celery salt

tomato juice

fino sherry

lemon juice

salt and
pepper

Tabasco
sauce

Worcestershire
sauce

creamed horseradish

1 Fill a bar glass or pitcher with cracked ice and add the vodka, sherry and tomato juice. Stir well.

2 Add the lemon juice, Tabasco and Worcestershire sauces and the horseradish to taste.

3 Add the celery salt, salt and pepper and stir until the pitcher has frosted and the contents are chilled.

4 Strain into a tall tumbler half filled with a couple of ice cubes.

5 Add a decorative stick of celery as a swizzle stick.

6 Thread a toothpick with olives and a cherry tomato, and place on the rim of the glass, then serve.

Apricot Bellini

This is a version of the famous apéritif served at Harry's Bar in Venice. Instead of the usual peaches and peach brandy, apricot nectar and apricot brandy make this a tempting variation.

VARIATION

Instead of apricots and apricot brandy, use fresh raspberries and raspberry-infused gin or syrup.

Serves 6–8

INGREDIENTS
3 apricots
2 teaspoons lemon juice
2 teaspoons sugar syrup
2 measures/3 tablespoons apricot
  brandy or peach schnapps
1 bottle *brut* champagne or dry
  sparkling wine, chilled

lemon juice

apricots

sparkling wine

apricot brandy

sugar syrup

1 Plunge the apricots into boiling water for 2 minutes to loosen the skins.

2 Peel and pit the apricots. Discard the pits and skin.

3 Process the apricot flesh with the lemon juice until you have a smooth purée. Sweeten to taste with sugar syrup, then strain.

4 Add the brandy or peach schnapps to the apricot nectar and stir together.

5 Divide the apricot nectar among chilled champagne flutes.

6 Finish the drinks with chilled champagne or sparkling wine.

Kir Lethale

The raisins for this cocktail can be soaked overnight in vodka.

Serves 6

INGREDIENTS
6 vodka-soaked raisins
2 tablespoons vodka or
  raisin vodka
3 measures/$4\frac{1}{2}$ tablespoons
  crème de cassis
1 bottle *brut* champagne or dry
  sparkling wine, chilled

crème de cassis

 *vodka-soaked raisins*

champagne

VARIATION

For Kir Framboise, use crème de framboise or raspberry syrup and raspberry-flavored vodka.

1 Place a vodka-soaked raisin at the bottom of each glass.

2 Add a teaspoon of vodka or the vodka from the steeped raisins, if using, to each glass.

3 Divide the crème de cassis equally among the glasses.

4 Before serving, finish the drinks with the champagne or sparkling wine.

Brandy Blazer

A warming after-dinner tipple, ideally served with fresh vanilla ice cream or caramelized oranges.

Serves 1

INGREDIENTS
1/2 orange
1 lemon
2 measures/3 tablespoons Cognac
1 sugar cube
1/2 measure/2 teaspoons Kahlúa
orange rind, threaded
    on to a cocktail stick, to decorate

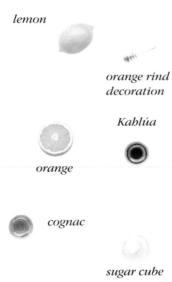

lemon

orange rind decoration

Kahlúa

orange

cognac

sugar cube

VARIATION

Pour the hot Cognac and Kahlúa mix into freshly brewed coffee and serve the drink black.

1 Pare the rind from the orange and lemon, removing and discarding as much of the white pith as possible.

2 Put the Cognac, sugar cube, lemon and orange rind in a small pan.

3 Heat gently, then remove from the heat, light a match and pass the flame close to the surface of the liquid. The alcohol will burn with a low, blue flame for about a minute. Blow out the flame.

4 Add the Kahlúa to the pan and strain into a heat-resistant liqueur glass. Decorate with a toothpick threaded with orange rind, then serve warm.

Long Island Iced Tea

A long, potent drink with an intoxicating effect, its strength is well disguised by the cola. For a simpler version, use equal quantities of rum, Cointreau, tequila and lemon juice and top up with cola.

Serves 1

INGREDIENTS
$^1/_2$ measure/2 teaspoons light rum
$^1/_2$ measure/2 teaspoons vodka
$^1/_2$ measure/2 teaspoons gin
$^1/_2$ measure/2 teaspoons Grand
  Marnier or Cointreau
1 measure/$1^1/_2$ tablespoons cold
  Earl Grey tea
juice of $^1/_2$ lemon
cola, chilled, to taste
slices of lemon and a large fresh
  mint sprig, to decorate

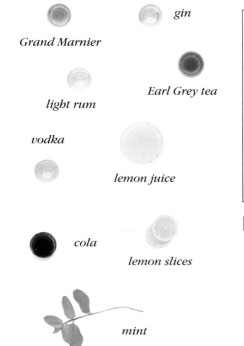

Grand Marnier

gin

light rum

Earl Grey tea

vodka

lemon juice

cola

lemon slices

mint

1 Fill a bar glass with cracked ice and add the rum, vodka, gin and Grand Marnier or Cointreau.

2 Add the cold Earl Grey tea to the spirits in the bar glass.

3 Stir well for 30 seconds to chill the spirits and the tea.

4 Add lemon juice to taste.

5 Strain into a highball glass filled with ice cubes and lemon.

6 Add chilled cola, to taste, then a fresh mint sprig to use as a swizzle stick.

Mint Julep

One of the oldest cocktails, this originated in the southern States of America. It's the classic accompaniment to the Kentucky Derby.

VARIATION
Add a splash of chilled soda water for a refreshing longer drink.

Serves 1

INGREDIENTS
1 tablespoon sugar
8–10 fresh mint leaves
1 tbsp hot water
2 measures/3 tablespoons bourbon
    or whiskey

hot water

mint leaves

sugar

bourbon

1 Place the sugar in a mortar or in a bar glass. Tear the mint leaves into small pieces and add them to the sugar.

2 Bruise the mint leaves with a pestle or use a muddler to release their flavor and color.

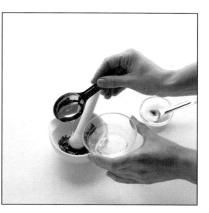

3 Add the hot water to the mint leaves and grind well together.

4 Spoon into a snifter glass or brandy balloon and half fill with crushed ice.

5 Add the bourbon or whiskey to the snifter glass.

6 Stir until the outside of the glass has frosted. Allow to stand for a couple of minutes until the ice melts slightly and dilutes the drink. Serve with straws, if desired.

Frozen Strawberry Daiquiri

A version of the Cuban original, which was made with only local Cuban rum, lime juice and sugar. When out of season, use drained, canned strawberries instead.

VARIATION

Substitute ¼ cup cream for the rum and brandy. Process in the blender and serve as a non-alcoholic daiquiri.

Serves 1

INGREDIENTS
4 strawberries
2 teaspoons fresh lime juice
1 measure/1½ tablespoons brandy
    or strawberry brandy
1 measure/1½ tablespoons
    light rum
dash of grenadine
strawberry and a fresh mint sprig,
    to decorate

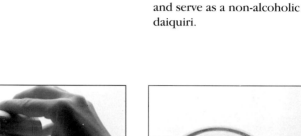

strawberries

lime juice

light rum

brandy

grenadine

mint sprig

1 Place ice cubes in a clean, folded dish towel and crush to a fine snow using a rolling pin or hammer.

2 Place the strawberries with the lime juice and brandy in a blender and process to a purée.

3 Add the light rum, grenadine and half a glass of finely crushed ice to the blender and process once more, to a smooth slush.

4 Pour the mixture into a well-chilled cocktail glass.

5 To decorate, remove the hull from the strawberry and replace with a small sprig of fresh mint.

6 Make a cut in the side of the strawberry and attach to the rim of the glass. Serve with a short straw, if liked.

Wilga Hill Boomerang

This sundowner is mixed in a large bar glass half filled with ice cubes, and is served super cold.

Serves 1

INGREDIENTS
1 measure/1¹/₂ tablespoons gin
¹/₄ measure/1 teaspoon dry
    vermouth
¹/₄ measure/1 teaspoon sweet
    vermouth
1 measure/1¹/₂ tablespoons
    apple juice
dash angostura bitters
2 dashes maraschino cherry juice
strip of orange rind and a
    maraschino cherry, to decorate

orange rind

apple juice

dry vermouth

*angostora
bitters*

*maraschino cherry
and juice*

gin

sweet vermouth

VARIATION

Omit the apple juice and serve over the rocks or, if preferred, substitute bourbon or Southern Comfort for the gin.

1 Pour the gin, dry and sweet vermouths and apple juice into a bar glass half filled with ice, and stir until the outside of the glass has frosted.

2 Add the angostura bitters and maraschino juice to the bottom of a cocktail glass and add ice cubes.

3 Strain the cocktail into a shorts tumbler.

4 Add the strip of orange rind and a maraschino cherry and serve.

Golden Start

A delicious and very drinkable mix of Galliano, orange, pineapple and cream of coconut.

Serves 1

INGREDIENTS
2 measures/3 tablespoons Galliano
1 measure/1½ tablespoons
   orange juice, chilled
1 measure/1½ tablespoons
   pineapple juice, chilled
1 measure/1½ tablespoons
   white or orange curaçao
1 measure/1½ tablespoons
   cream of coconut
2 tablespoons pineapple juice and
   1 ounce sugar, to decorate

white curaçao   *Galliano*

sugar

orange juice

pineapple juice

cream of coconut

VARIATION

For an extra tropical twist, substitute light crème de cacao for the curaçao.

1 Put the Galliano, orange and pineapple juices and curaçao in a blender and process together.

2 Add the cream of coconut with a tablespoon of fine ice snow and process until smooth and frothy.

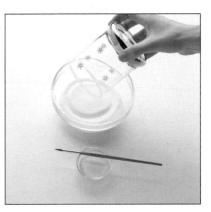

3 Rub the rim of the cocktail glass with pineapple juice and invert the glass into a saucer of sugar to frost the rim.

4 Pour the cocktail into the prepared glass while still frothy.

Sea Dog

A long whiskey drink with a citrus twist. For a sweeter drink, add another sugar cube; if including Drambuie, use only one.

VARIATION

Use gin in place of the whiskey and Pimms in place of the Benedictine.

Serves 1

INGREDIENTS
1–2 sugar cubes
2 dashes angostura bitters
2 oranges wedges
2 lemon wedges
$^2/_3$ measure/1 tablespoon whiskey or
    Drambuie
1 measure/$1^1/_2$ tablespoons
    Benedictine
2 measures/3 tablespoons
    soda water, chilled, or to taste
maraschino cherry, to decorate

Benedictine

sugar cubes

angostura bitters

whiskey

orange wedges

soda water

lemon wedges

maraschino cherry

1 Put the sugar cube at the bottom of a Collins glass, add the bitters and allow to soak into the sugar cube.

2 Add the orange and lemon wedges and, using a muddler, press the juices from the fruit.

3 Fill the glass with cracked ice.

4 Add the whiskey and the Benedictine and mix together well with a swizzle stick for 20 seconds.

5 Add chilled soda water to taste.

6 Serve with the muddler, so that more juice can be pressed from the fruit, according to personal taste; decorate with a maraschino cherry.

Harvey Wallbanger

The next step up from a Screwdriver – with a dash of Galliano. Those who prefer a stronger cocktail should add an extra measure of vodka.

VARIATION

Combine the orange juice and vodka with a splash of ginger wine, pour into a glass and slowly pour the Galliano on top.

Serves 1

INGREDIENTS
1 measure/1½ tablespoons vodka
²/₃ measure/1 tablespoon Galliano
7 measures/²/₃ cup
   orange juice
½ small orange, to decorate

orange juice

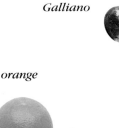

Galliano

orange

vodka

1 Pour the vodka, Galliano and orange juice into a bar glass of ice.

2 Mix the cocktail and ice for 30 seconds to chill it well.

3 Using a canelle knife, take a series of strips of rind off the orange, running from the top to the bottom of the fruit.

4 Use a small, sharp knife to cut the orange evenly and thinly into slices.

5 Cut the orange slices in half and wedge them between cracked ice in a highball glass.

6 Strain the chilled cocktail into the prepared glass.

Apple Sour

For those with concerns about eating raw egg, this variation on a Brandy Sour can be made without the egg white. Applejack or apple schnapps also works well, in place of the Calvados.

Serves 1

INGREDIENTS
1 measure/1¹/₂ tablespoons
 Calvados
²/₃ measure/1 tablespoon lemon
 juice
1 teaspoon sugar
1 dash angostura bitters
1 egg white
red and green apple slices and
 fresh lemon juice, to decorate

egg white

lemon juice

sugar

angostura bitters   *red and green apples*

Calvados

1 Add the Calvados, lemon juice and sugar into a shaker of ice, with the angostura bitters and egg white.

2 Shake together for 30 seconds.

VARIATION
Sours can also be made with Amaretto or tequila; add a splash of raspberry syrup or port to the glass just before serving.

3 Strain the cocktail into a tumbler of cracked ice.

4 Dip the red and green apple slices in lemon juice. Decorate the cocktail with the apple slices threaded onto a bamboo skewer.

East India

This short and elegant drink can be served as an apéritif, dressed with a twist of lime rind and a maraschino cherry.

Serves 1

INGREDIENTS
²/₃ measure/1 tablespoon brandy
2 dashes white curaçao
2 dashes pineapple juice
2 dashes angostura bitters
1 lime and a maraschino cherry,
   to decorate

 maraschino cherry

lime

angostura bitters

white curaçao

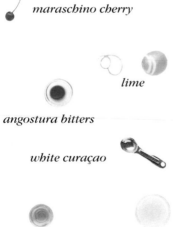

brandy   *pineapple juice*

VARIATION

Mix equal quantities of dry vermouth and dry sherry with angostura bitters and serve on the rocks.

1 Put the brandy, curaçao, pineapple juice and bitters into a bar glass of ice.

2 Stir the cocktail well for about 20 seconds until chilled and strain into a squat tumbler over the rocks.

3 Using a canelle knife, remove a piece of rind from a lime.

4 Tightly twist into a coil, hold for a few seconds, and add to the drink with a maraschino cherry.

Planters Punch

This long, refreshing, old colonial drink originates from the sugar plantations that are dotted throughout the West Indies.

VARIATION

Add 1 measure/1¹/₂ tablespoons cold Assam tea, for a different tang.

Serves 1

INGREDIENTS
1 measure/1¹/₂ tablespoons
   fresh lime juice
1 measure/1¹/₂ tablespoons orange
   juice (optional)
2 measures/3 tablespoons dark rum
2 teaspoons grenadine
1 dash angostura bitters
soda water or lemonade, chilled
peach slices and a Cape
   gooseberry, to decorate

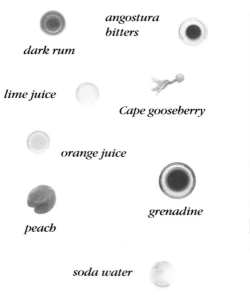

dark rum

angostura bitters

lime juice

Cape gooseberry

orange juice

grenadine

peach

soda water

1 Squeeze the lime and orange juices and add to a bar glass of ice.

2 Add the dark rum and the grenadine and mix together for about 20 seconds.

3 Add a dash of bitters to the bottom of a tumbler of decorative ice cubes.

4 Strain the rum and grenadine mixture into the chilled tumbler.

5 Finish with plenty of chilled soda water or lemonade.

6 Decorate with peach slices and a Cape gooseberry.

Singapore Sling

The origins of this old-fashioned thirst quencher lie far away to the east.

VARIATION

Substitute Benedictine for the Cointreau for a Straits Sling. Add ginger beer instead of soda water for a Raffles Bar Sling.

Serves 1

INGREDIENTS
2 measures/3 tablespoons gin
juice of 1 lemon
1 teaspoon sugar
soda water, chilled
²/₃ measure/1 tablespoon Cointreau
²/₃ measure/1 tablespoon cherry
   brandy
1 lemon and 1 black cherry, to
   decorate

black cherry

lemon

gin

Cointreau

cherry brandy

sugar

soda water

1 Pour the gin into a bar glass of ice and mix with the lemon juice and sugar.

2 Strain the cocktail into a tumbler full of cracked ice.

3 Finish the cocktail with chilled soda water to taste.

4 Add the Cointreau and the cherry brandy, but do not stir.

5 To decorate, use a vegetable peeler or sharp knife to cut a long piece of rind round the lemon.

6 Place the lemon rind in the glass. Thread the cherry onto two toothpicks and add to the rim of the glass.

Kew Pimms

A very drinkable concoction of sweet vermouth, curaçao, vodka, gin and cherry brandy served over summer fruit.

VARIATION

For a longer drink, finish with champagne, sparkling wine or tonic water.

Serves 1

INGREDIENTS

1 measure/1½ tablespoons sweet vermouth
1 measure/1½ tablespoons orange curaçao
⅔ measure/1 tablespoon vodka
⅔ measure/1 tablespoon gin
⅔ measure/1 tablespoon cherry brandy
assorted soft summer fruits
1–2 dashes angostura bitters
2 measures/3 tablespoons American dry ginger ale, chilled
2 measures/3 tablespoons lemonade, chilled
1 lemon, to decorate
fresh lemon balm or mint leaves, to decorate

lemon balm

lemon

orange curaçao

vodka

summer fruits

angostura bitters

sweet vermouth

gin

cherry brandy

lemonade

dry ginger ale

1 Measure the vermouth, curaçao, vodka, gin and cherry brandy into a bar glass of ice and stir well to chill.

2 Strain into a tall highball glass full of ice cubes and the summer fruits.

3 Add the bitters and then pour in equal quantities of chilled ginger ale and lemonade to taste.

4 To make lemon triangles, pare a thin piece of lemon rind from the lemon.

5 Cut the rind into a rectangle and cut a slit three-quarters of the way across the lemon rind. Turn the rectangle and repeat from the other side.

6 Twist to form a triangle, crossing the ends to secure them. Add to the drink with lemon balm or mint leaves.